Make it Happen
in the Real World

Make it Happen in the Real World

◆

A Practical Guide to Getting Your Finances in Order for Everyday People

Tiffanie

iUniverse, Inc.
New York Lincoln Shanghai

Make it Happen in the Real World
A Practical Guide to Getting Your Finances in Order for Everyday People

iUniverse books may be ordered through booksellers or by contacting:

iUniverse
2021 Pine Lake Road, Suite 100
Lincoln, NE 68512
www.iuniverse.com
1-800-Authors (1-800-288-4677)

Because of the dynamic nature of the Internet, any Web addresses or links contained in this book may have changed since publication and may no longer be valid.

The information, ideas, and suggestions in this book are not intended to render professional advice. Before following any suggestions contained in this book, you should consult your personal accountant or other financial advisor. Neither the author nor the publisher shall be liable or responsible for any loss or damage allegedly arising as a consequence of your use or application of any information or suggestions in this book.

ISBN: 978-0-595-46416-6 (pbk)
ISBN: 978-0-595-90710-6 (ebk)

Printed in the United States of America

To my Lord and Savior, Jesus Christ, and my parents, family, friends, and ancestors.

Contents

Acknowledgments

In my journey of promise and purpose, I am grateful to an array of wonderful, caring individuals. I am eternally grateful for my Lord and Savior, Jesus Christ, and my parents, family, and friends, who motivated me through the good and challenging times. I would also like to thank my ancestors for their prayers, struggles, and accomplishments for future generations. Thank you!

My Testimony

Dear Jesus,

There are no words that can express how thankful I am for you loving me everyday. Although I grew up in the church as a child, I did not truly understand and have real faith until now. I know I have a long way to go, but I do not want my blessings to be unnoticed. I want the world to know that whatever they have seen or been through in their life, they are truly blessed and have a purpose. I am so thankful that I truly understand Proverbs 3: 5–6. Thank you Jesus!

At the age of seven, with the ugly divorce of my parents where I witnessed my father shooting at my mother six times and not one bullet touches her was indescribable. At that moment, I knew you are in control and have all power. Thank you Jesus!

At the age of eight, starting over from humble beginnings, I gave you my life and made you my Lord and Savior. At that moment, you provided me with an immeasurable extended family of love and friendship. Thank you Jesus!

As a teenager, you healed my heart to start fresh relationships with my biological father as well as my step father. I was not the best teenager in the world, but you and others were definitely praying to keep me from harms way. To know where I could have been … Thank you Jesus!

As a young adult, I can look back and say thank you for my health, college struggles of working two jobs, having student loans, and not being too proud to eat Ramon noodles (in fact, I use to image I was eating steak and potatoes). Those were challenging times where I thought I would lose my mind, but you stood by my side and even provided me with countless positive friends and second mothers and fathers who made me a stronger person. At that moment I truly understood Proverbs 27:17. Thank you Jesus!

Today, I thank you for humbling me for my purpose in life. Thank you for telling me to trust you, move 600 miles away from home, get a part time job and seek my career position. I can look back and see that by walking by faith, everything was right on time. I did not understand until now why my middle name was Grace and momma's favorite verse was Psalm 100. For Grace is of favor, mercy, and moral strength where you have blessed me forever (Psalm 45:2) and Psalm 100 is Psalm of praise for all generations. The previous generations broke some strong holds, but future generations have a financial strong hold to break. Just as I was eight years old, I made you my Lord & Savior, and I know the devil has peaked into my future and has started to work overtime with me, but I want to let him know to get out of my way, my cup runnith over. Thank you Jesus!

Love,
Tiffanie

Preface

Well, here is another self-help, money-coach, get-out-of-debt theory book; however, this book has a twist. It is a practical, cut-and-dry guide on how to save and make money for the everyday person. Keep a pen handy to underline information that is new to you. Read with an open mind, and try to expand your normal patterns of thinking. After one year of financial change, I would like to hear your comments (good or bad). Please e-mail me at anchored4generations@yahoo.com.

This is just a baby step toward becoming financially savvy, so I encourage everyone who needs financial change to read various financial books by America's best-selling authors: Glinda Bridgforth and Gail Perry-Mason, Lynnette Khalfani, Robert Kiyosaki, Suze Orman, and Dave Ramsey.

I am confident that as a quick reference for practical information on how to survive in the real world—whether you were recently downsized, laid off, fired, living paycheck-to-paycheck, starting a new life on your own, or still unemployed after graduation—this information will be beneficial for your future. I have divided this book into three "real-life" parts:

"Part I: The Beginning" describes your current situation.
"Part II: The Breakthrough" identifies financial priorities and helps you establish a budget.

"Part III: The Results" provides further tips and resources for financial change.

Please remember to be open to new ways of thinking and seeing the world, so you can be creative and use my suggestions to assist you in developing your own solutions. Be aware that in some cases, you will need to make your financial decisions by following up with proper documentation, consulting your financial advisor or accountant, or visit www.irs.gov.

Please note that this book is a source of general advice only. Please consult with your financial advisor before making any major financial decisions. This book is sponsored by Anchored 4 Generations, LLC, which is not responsible for any losses, damages, or claims that may result from your financial decisions.

Part I

The Beginning

Chapter 1

The Real World

Remember graduation? You were in the class of XX, your future was bright, you were on top of the world, you were going to make a difference, and you partied like you never had before. Then you woke up, and graduation was just a memory. After all the studying of theories, solving equations, and critical thinking, you wondered why your parents and professors had failed to tell you how to live in the real world. Then you realized it was not that they had failed; it was that the world had changed drastically. So here you are, struggling to live in this world of corporate scandals, reduced job security, and increased education debt. Within months you find that you are overeducated for a minimum-wage job to pay off student loans and too inexperienced to start a career. With a six-month grace period before you must begin repaying your student loans, the real world does not seem as bright.

So what do you do? You do the best you can and pay what you can, when you can. The reality is that you need to learn how to live within your budget and establish a budget now! What is "living within your budget"? Living within your budget is a way to ensure that what you spend each month is less than what you make. Only creating a budget before you create the bills will allow you to understand your limitations. Stop saying, "I make $XX,XXX a year, so I can afford $19.95 a month for Internet, $39.95 a month for cable," and so on. After surcharges and taxes, that totals over $60, and guess what—with a few more bills like that, you will not be able to afford them all, not to mention you are starting bad habits of not living within your budget.

How do you create a budget? Every situation is different, and there are thousands of budget templates out there, so create your own budget based on percentages of your net income. The guideline is to establish percentages for expenses without going over 100 percent. Write down what you can afford in each category. For example, if your net income is $2,000 a month, 10 percent of $2,000 is $200 to go toward tithes and charity monthly. Of course, some percentages vary, but you can determine whether you are living within your budget. Use the Net column to establish what you can afford to pay and the Actual column to record what you currently pay. Refer to appendix 1 for a complete example.

		Net (monthly)	Actual (monthly)
Tithes and Charity	10%	_____	_____
Savings	10%	_____	_____
Housing	30%	_____	_____
Utilities and Cell phone	10%	_____	_____
Insurance (Car and Health)	5%	_____	_____
Transportation (Auto)	10%	_____	_____
Debt (e.g., Student Loans)	15%	_____	_____
Food	5%	_____	_____
Personal Care	2.5%	_____	_____

		Net (monthly)	Actual (monthly)
Recreation and Clothing	2.5%	_____	_____
Total	100%	_____	_____

I hope this information has opened your eyes so you understand that it is okay if you cannot afford that $19.95 monthly Internet bill. You should be proud of your education—it's quite an accomplishment—but just because you graduated does not mean that you can afford all the luxuries in life right now; you still have to pay your dues in life. So wake up before it is twenty years later, you are married with children, your parents are living with you, and you are on the verge of a foreclosure because your company is under investigation for corporate scandals, which, along with your health conditions, put your job security uncertain. I know that is a little extreme, but life happens.

If there is one thing I want you to take from this book, it is that you should seek the information for yourself. Please, please, please read the fine print before you sign. Please, please, please seek a second opinion; do not just take one person's word for it. This is your life, so take care of it.

Chapter 2

I Have to Eat

Your eating habits will determine your long-term health and financial well-being. America is undergoing several health crises, including high blood pressure, diabetes, and heart disease. With what we know now, how can we not change our eating habits? For example, when you take medication for high blood pressure, it is essential to change your eating habits. Wake up! Your body is an amazing blessing from God, so take care of it. I am not a doctor or dietitian; however, I recommend reading *Dr. Ro's Ten Secrets to Livin' Healthy* by Rovenia M. Brock, PhD; *MediSin* by Scott Whitaker and Jose Fleming; and *Prescription for Nutritional Healing* by Phyllis A. Balch, CNC.

If you do not want to think about what your eating habits are doing to your body, then just think about your typical day and how much your eating habits affect your budget. We run out the door without eating breakfast, so we go to a fast-food chain restaurant. Of course, we left lunch in the refrigerator, so we are forced to buy more fast food, not to mention grab something on the way home. Within one day you can spend $4.79 on breakfast, $6.49 on lunch, and $8.24 on dinner, and eat enough fried foods to increase your health risk, with additional love handles that will take years to get off.

People do not realize how much money they spend on food. Take your place of employment, for example; observe upper management. Do they go out to eat every day? If they do, I *guarantee* they are putting their lunches on their business expense reports, and they make more than you. How much do you spend? Collect all the fast food receipts, and look at your last grocery receipt. How much would you spend if you reduced the fast food visits, bought generic brands at the grocery store, or used coupons? Speaking of generic brands, why are we so obligated to purchase name-brand foods? FYI: a large percentage of the name-brand foods have the same ingredients and/or are processed by the same manufacturers. Reevaluate your grocery shopping, food intake, and related habits. A later chapter ("Chapter 7: Be Creative") contains various other ways to reduce your grocery bill. In some cases, you can get paid to eat.

To get you started, here are a few ways to avoid fast food: use reminders so you do not forget to take food with you. For example, place a "Don't forget the lunch" note on the front door. Of course, the note does not have to be there forever—just long enough so you get in the habit of taking your lunch. Or place your keys or briefcase by the refrigerator as a reminder. Stock up on food or cook enough for the week, and keep healthy foods at work and in your car for breakfast or snacks; this comes in handy when you are stuck in traffic or have an errand to run after work.

Chapter 3

I Don't Pay My Bills;
I Pay on My Bills

So you entered the real world and established your own budget, but guess what happened? Gas prices rose out of control, credit card companies increased their minimum payments, and your company's health care benefit premiums increased. Within one billing period, you find yourself trying to figure out what happened. So you are paying all your bills with little or nothing left over. You cannot pay the entire balance of some bills. At this moment, you are not paying your bills; you are merely paying on your bills.

If you get another part-time job, most of your earnings will be taken by the cost of gas to get there, additional taxes, and the food you buy on the way there. What do you do? You must get creative in seeking information.

Unfortunately, people often let their finances get completely out of control before they implement change. "Part II: The Breakthrough" will focus on identifying the realities of many of our lives and how to change if you are serious. If you are not sick and tired of your out-of-control finances yet, here is a reality check: Refer to appendix 2, and fill out the "Sick and Tired" form. Write down your net income and all your bills with their interest rates and monthly payments. Do the math. Are you paying your bills, or are you merely paying on your bills? Before you move to part 2, you have to be sick and tired of living this way. Are you? If not, allow someone else to borrow this book until you are.

"Part III: The Results" provides further tips and resources for financial change. No sugarcoating or dancing around the answer: it is practical, cut-and-dry advice on how to save and make money for the everyday person.

Part II

The Breakthrough

Chapter 4

Priorities

The breakthrough deprograms your skewed priorities by showing you how quickly one can get stuck in the "I Don't Pay My Bills; I Pay on My Bills" scenario and showing you how to eat and shop without killing your body and pocket. This world has programmed millions to get it now and pay it later; unfortunately, paying it later never seems to pay it off. To find out if you are in trouble, read a few of these statements to see if you fit in any of these categories.

- You play your numbers once a week, hoping to win the lottery and retire, and do not currently have a financial plan for retirement. The reality is that if you invest a dollar a week for the time it takes to reach retirement, you can have a modest nest egg instead of stacks of losing lottery tickets. Where are your priorities?

- You get your eyebrows, hair, manicure, and pedicure done regularly, but you cannot pay the full balance of your utility bills. Where are your priorities?

- You are wearing a $100 pair of shoes and a $50 belt and carrying a $200 purse, but you can not match the total in savings. Where are your priorities?

- You go to the mall and spend $10 or more at the food court but have no food in the refrigerator. Where are your priorities?

- You have health insurance but will not go for a regular checkup because you cannot afford the co-pay. Where are your priorities?

- You buy the latest DVD or video game every week but do not have gas in the car to get to work. Where are your priorities?

- You have rims that cost more than your car. Where are your priorities?

- Your child wears the latest name-brand clothes, but you cannot pay for their school supplies. Where are your priorities?

- You can buy cigarettes, go to the movies, go out to the clubs, and socialize as much as you like, but you cannot pay your tithes. Where are your priorities?

- You have cable and Internet but cannot afford to get oil changes for your car, so you wait until your car breaks down, which forces you to spend your entire income tax check to get it fixed. Where are your priorities?

- You have the latest cell phone, but you cannot pay the bill. Where are your priorities?

- The only place you can buy a car is at a "your job is your credit" car dealership, where they talk loud and have biweekly payment plans to insult your intelligence. (Why are they yelling? And just because it is $200 every two weeks, it is still a $400 per month car payment.) Where are your priorities?

- Because your credit score was ruined by extensive debt, you have to pay a deposit whenever you open an account. Where are your priorities?

- You can save and plan to go on cruises, but you cannot pay off a credit card bill in the same amount. Where are your priorities?

- When you get paid, you go out to the movies or buy yourself something. Then you go home to balance your checkbook, and you are baffled because you did not budget before you spent the money. Where are your priorities?

- You live in a place you can barely afford because you need plenty of closet room for your name-brand clothing. Where are your priorities?

- You use a credit card to look flashy, but you cannot pay the balance at the end of the month. Where are your priorities?

- You do not claim yourself on your taxes so you can have a bigger income tax check. The reality is that you are allowing the government to hold your money interest-free, while your credit cards are collecting an interest rate. Where are your priorities?

Ouch! The truth hurts, and we can make all the excuses in the world, but the reality is that if you fit into the above categories, you are drowning.

Please do not think you are battling this alone, and please do not think everyone else is doing so well. Just because someone makes $60,000 a year does not mean they are better off than someone who makes $30,000 a year. This is just one of the few things in life people can hide. So, honestly, do you have to have it right now? Will your ears fall off if you do not buy those earrings? Will your thumbs disappear if you do not buy that video game? Will your eyeballs come out of their sockets if you do not see the latest movie? Who cares what people say? They are not paying your bills.

As future parents, are your children really going to remember the thousands of dollars you spent on Christmas or that expensive birthday party when they were three years old? What your children will remember is when you tell them you do not have any money for them to go to college. That will be tattooed in their brains and sometimes affect their destinies.

So what do you do? You start looking at everything you do differently; you start thinking about new and unusual solutions; you become more creative in seeking information—you become a person on a mission.

Chapter 5

Nobody Told Me,
or I Didn't Know

As you experience your Breakthrough, look back at the budget you created in chapter 1. Did you determine how much you can really afford for your expenses? Let's get informed about the following areas: tithes and charitable donations, savings, housing, utilities and cell phone, insurance (car and health), transportation (auto), debt (e.g., student loans), food, personal care, recreation and clothing.

Nobody told me, or I didn't know ...

Tithes and Charitable Donations are tax deductible, so write a check and get a receipt; this will help you lower your tax bracket. Make sure you are a member of the church, and make sure you have the tax ID number of the charity.

Savings. Pay yourself first, and do not put all your eggs in one basket. Have a variety of funds for retirement. Take advantage of your company's 401(k) plan. Think about this: whenever you contribute to your 401(k), that amount is subtracted from your earned income. The amount you contribute may put you in a lower tax bracket, and your company is matching what you contribute, so that is *free money!*

Your 401(k) is for your retirement; however, a lot of people borrow from their 401(k) during financial hardships. As long as you borrow from your 401(k) and pay it back with a small interest rate, it is considered a loan, and you will not be penalized by the IRS.

Contributing to an IRA (Individual Retirement Account) can be another huge asset during emergencies. With a Roth IRA, money is contributed after taxes are taken out of your paycheck, so when you take your money out of your IRA at age fifty-nine and a half, the money is tax free. During financial hardships, you can take out the entire amount you put in (not the interest accrued on the account) as long as you pay it back within sixty days. You can do this only once a year. Check with your credit union for more information. That's right, *credit union*—these have fewer fees and higher interest rates in most cases. Those options are cheaper than any credit card. You do not have to have thousands of dollars to start your IRA; you can start with as little as $5 at some credit unions and contribute when you can.

Okay, saving for retirement is one thing, but how do you get the most out of your savings for emergencies? Certificates of Deposits (CDs). CDs offer higher rates of return than most comparable investments in exchange for letting the bank hold the invested money for short or medium length of time until the certificate matures. CDs are low risk and FDIC insured and offered by credit unions and banks. The investment in a CD will allow you to collect more interest than a savings account; however, you must wait until the CD matures, which varies from three months to six years. Once your CD matures, you are welcome to cash in with no penalty. Check with your credit union, or visit www.investopedia. com/terms/c/certificateofdeposit.asp for more information.

Do you have absolutely no savings for your child's college education? Do you buy your food at a grocery store to feed your child? Do you buy gas to go to work? Do you shop at major department stores to buy school clothes? Then guess what: you can start paying for college now. Get a free membership to www.upromise.com, and every time you purchase certain everyday items, a percentage will go into your child's account. Every little bit helps. You can also sign up family and friends to contribute to your child's education. Don't have any children? Set up an account for your sibling, cousin, niece, nephew, godchild, or a child you mentor. Invest in their future.

Housing. First apartment? Just bought a house? Transferring to a new city? Whatever your situation, take advantage of the offers available to you. Go to your local post office, and pick up a moving packet. Inside, you will find all kinds of moving coupons. Trying to save to purchase a home, while rent keeps going up? Go to your apartment manager and explain that you are saving up for a home and you have been a good renter (you always pay on time and cause no trouble), so keeping the rent at the same amount would help you financially. If the manager says no, ask him or her to meet you halfway. For example, if rent is $550 and it is going up to $600, ask if it can be increased to $575 instead. If the manager still says no, go to his or her boss. If you are temporarily renting, and you really want a certain apartment, but it costs more than you can afford, tell them their competitor's special offer is cheaper, and ask if they can match it. Of course, follow up with a certified letter. Refer to appendix 3.

Do not get comfortable paying for someone else's mortgage, or someone else's vacation—that is exactly what you are doing if you are renting an apartment or house. Stop making the excuse that the reason you have not bought anything is you want to buy something you really want. Be honest; do you know anyone who bought their dream home the first time around? I only know one person who was able to do that.

Smart homeowners buy what they can afford comfortably and stack their money. After all, homeowners claim approximately 95 percent of the mortgage interest on their taxes for the first couple of years. What does that mean? If your rent is $800 a month, you are spending $9,600 per year. If you own a home, condo, or townhouse with a mortgage of $800 a month, you are spending $9,600 per year, of which 95 percent will be claimed on your taxes. That is $9,120 you can claim on your taxes. Still have excuses for why you are not a homeowner? Of course, there are many legitimate reasons you may not be able to purchase a home right away, but let's not turn it into a five-year-plus excuse. Just think of all the money you are throwing away.

If you are a homeowner … congratulations! If you did not have the 20 percent down payment, you may have to pay private mortgage insurance (PMI) until 80 percent of the property is paid for. The Homeowner's Protection Act (HPA) passed in 1999; state lenders must cancel mortgage insurance when the loan-to-value ratio reaches 22 percent. However, in two years, if your property value increases over that 80 percent, and you have not been late on any mortgage payments, you may request to have your PMI canceled. Please note that PMI is a financial security that insures lenders against loss if the homeowner defaults on a mortgage. If the homeowner defaults and the lender takes the title to the property, the mortgage insurer reduces or eliminates the loss to the lender (sharing the risk of lending the money to the borrower).

Understand that canceling your PMI will save you hundreds, even thousands of dollars. The bank or credit union will make its final attempt to get as much money out of you as possible. Be prepared to pay for a nonrefundable appraisal to confirm the current value of the property. Make sure the housing market is advantageous to the seller and that similar homes in the area reflect the bank's value requirement. It may take up to four weeks to complete the appraisal and another four weeks for the bank or credit union to cancel the PMI. You will not break even for a few months, but realize that you are saving an enormous amount over time. Refer to the example below:

You purchased your home for $100,000 (appraised at $100,000) at a 5.75 percent interest rate for thirty years. Refer to the table below. Depending on the location, your mortgage, property tax, and PMI will be approximately $904. After two years, your balance on your home will be approximately $97,500. Within two years your neighborhood has opened a variety of new restaurants, making the value of your home $120,000. If you do nothing and continue to pay $100 for your PMI until you pay 80 percent of the $100,000 loan, you will have paid a total of $10,800 over the course of nine years. However, if the value of your home increased more than 20 percent after two years, the PMI would be cancelled, saving you a total of $8,400.

Principal and Interest	$584
Taxes and Insurance	$250
Mortgage Insurance	$70
Total Payment	$904

Please note that this is just a general example to explain reduced mortgage payment options. Mortgage insurance premiums vary. Refer to appendix 4 to request what is needed to cancel your PMI for your home.

Utilities and Cell Phone. Saving energy can save the planet and your pocket. Visit www.energysavers.gov for your own free energy savings brochure and CD. If you are a homeowner, saving on your monthly utilities can also benefit your taxes. Visit www.energy.gov/taxbreaks.htm for tax break information.

Did you get your utilities based on a special or promotion? Remember that there will always be another special or sale. Have you ever called the utility company and asked what the mysterious fees on your bill are for? Well, you should; you are paying taxes on those fees, and within a year you will be spending $20 or more for nothing! Reevaluate your needs: it may be more beneficial to purchase an answering machine for a one-time $20 in lieu of paying $4.95 a month for voicemail ($59 or more a year). I know an answering machine is so old-school, but it's money well spent if it does not consume too much energy.

Insurance (Car and Health). Medical expenses are out of control even when you have insurance. If you have difficulty paying your medical bills, see if you qualify for hospital assistance.

Are you obligated to keep the same insurance company? Get a quote from other companies, and make your insurance company work for your business. Yes, it will take a few minutes online to get a quote, but it may save you money. Do you have a separate road service besides your car insurance? Well, your car insurance company can supply the same towing service for a fraction of the cost. Are you in school with good grades? Are you over twenty-five years old? You can even get a discount for having multiple policies (e.g., car and home); just ask for it.

When it comes to deductibles, yes, initially it makes sense to pay $250 versus $500 whenever an accident occurs; however, you must look past the surface. If you have $500 for emergencies in a savings or money market account or a CD, then choose the $500 deductible, which will save you money on your insurance yearly. That way you can pay less in insurance and gain compound interest in your account.

Transportation (Auto). The twenty-first century has brought a new method of competition: banks and credit unions fight for your business. Visit www.lendingtree.com, www.bankrate.com, or your current bank or credit union. When interest rates are lower and your credit score increases, refinance your loans to save money.

The price of gas is already out of control; why settle for the over-priced gas in your neighborhood? Purchase your gas where it is cheaper: near your church, job, or school. Learn how to do your own oil changes, or go to a vocational school, which may allow students to change your oil for a discounted fee. Carpool and plan your trips; check to see if the Department of Transportation (DOT) offers funding for taking a different route during road construction. Visit various Web sites for travel coupons. If you get your car maintenance done at a car dealership, ask for a complimentary car wash. The worst thing they can say is no.

Debt (e.g., Student Loans). Consolidate your loans into one low interest rate. During financial hardship, place your student loans in forbearance. If you volunteer, find out whether you are eligible for loan forgiveness by checking the Web site http://www.finaid.org/loans/forgiveness.phtml. You may also be eligible if you are a teacher or child care provider in a low-income community. Do not forget that if you fall into a particular income bracket you can take a tax deduction for the interest of student loans for the life of the loans.

As for credit cards, transfer high credit card interest rates to 0 percent interest rate cards; *please read the fine print regarding annual activation and payment option fees.* Be creative to pay off this bad debt (see part III). In some cases, you may even be able to repair your credit within six months to a year, so go to www.freecreditreport.com to review reports from all three credit bureaus (in numerous states, everyone is entitled to at least one free credit report per year).

Food. Buy generic brands. Cook more often. And use coupons when you grocery shop. Going out to dinner with friends? Request to have lunch instead of dinner. If you must enjoy the night life, order a lunch serving size; it is cheaper. If you must eat out, eat half now and the other half later. Refer to "Chapter 7: Be Creative."

Personal Care. Free hygiene samples are convenient when traveling because the samples are smaller; buy generic hygiene products or go online to order free samples. Unfortunately, free samples vary with the promotion. If you would like to know where to get free samples, visit my Web site at www.anchored4generations.com under book freebies to see the latest Web sites I normally use. Also refer to "Chapter 7: Be Creative."

Recreation and Clothing. Take off-peak vacations; use your college ID for discounts (e.g., movies); shop at consignment shops, thrift stores, yard sales, or eBay; share clothes with friends who will wash and return them, and shop out of season. Go to estate sales for furniture.

With my experience reading the newspaper, watching early morning shows, and working in retail when I was a teenager, I learned the best times to make certain purchases. During the winter months of January and February, the holiday season is over, so take advantage of the Christmas clearance sales for items such as holiday decorations. This is also a good time to purchase home décor for the bedroom, such as linens. Calendars, jewelry, and coats are also good purchases during this time.

As you enter the spring months of March, April, and May, take advantage of deals on air conditioners, frozen foods, and electronics. In most cases, March is the end of the fiscal year for Japan; therefore, electronics will be 20 percent off or more. Take advantage of prices on carpet, rugs, and painting supplies. The month of May also provides sales for spring bedding, housewares, and spring clothing.

The summer months are a time of preparation for upcoming holiday events. During the months of June, July, and August, you will often find discounts for the following: weddings, Father's Day tools, menswear, sporting goods, electronics, and major appliances (e.g., refrigerators, washers, and dryers). In most cases, August is the end of the fiscal year for cars (new models come out in August); therefore, purchasing a vehicle will be to a consumer's advantage. Other sale items consist of patio furniture, grills, and swimwear.

The fall months of September, October, and November prepare you for a new season. September and October provide discounts for wedding items, air conditioners, golf equipment, and school supplies. November is a good time to purchase blankets and quilts. The fall is also the off-season for real estate.

The month of December has a variety of sales for the holidays on goods like cell phones, women's shoes, clothing, baby furniture, and more.

Whenever you decide to shop for items, pay attention to when there is a sale and shop the night before. In most cases, the sale is in the system the day before the sale after 5:30 PM. to avoid browsing in line shop at the competitor's location to avoid the crowd.

So far you have numerous ways to reduce your monthly bills. Refer to appendix 5 now for a chart that will help you trim unnecessary expenses.

Chapter 6

Use Your Resources

I hope you have learned something new from the previous chapters. If you would like to save even more, this is where we get more creative and use our resources. Everybody knows somebody in every industry. For example, my cousin is a nurse and my uncle is a mechanic; the list goes on and on, and you better believe I call them all the time to ask about health and car problems. Think about it; the people you know will eliminate the runaround and give you valuable advice, because they love you and want the best for you. If they do not know, they know someone who does.

What knowledge do you have? Where do you work? What have you learned over the years? Look at your bills. Do you know anyone who works at the telephone company? What items can be taken off of your bills? Do you know a mechanic? How much will it really cost to get your car fixed?

This book references many Web sites. Stop making excuses: "I don't have a computer," "I don't have the money to buy all those books you referenced," or "I don't have the money to check my credit report." You've already seen how to get a free credit report. For the books and Web sites, the answer is simple. Taxes are taken out of your paycheck each pay period, so get your money's worth by using the resources that those taxes make available. If you do not have a computer, go to the library or your state or county office. If you do not have the money to buy the books I reference, go to the library and check them out.

In some cases, you may even be able to repair your credit within six months to a year, so go to www.freecreditreport.com to review reports from all three credit reporting agencies (in numerous states, everyone is entitled to at least one free credit report per year).

Employment. Just graduated? Seeking an entry-level position with no experience can be very challenging. Looking for employment is a job itself, but the Internet has made seeking a career a lot easier. This is your life; you worked hard for that degree, so if you want a career, expect to submit numerous resumes, make hundreds of phone calls, and look forward to a lot of e-mail correspondence and interviews. Be prepared to move to a different city. Go get it.

Use your resources. Start with your university's career center and attend the university career fairs as well as other career fairs in your area. Get a headhunter, network with alumni, join the career association, network with church members, volunteer with similar career interest groups, talk to your coworkers and friends, and sign up with the various job Web sites, such as www.monster.com.

Just because you did not get the position you really wanted at the huge company does not mean your life is over. Be creative. What other businesses does that company have partnerships with? For example, if you are seeking a position in communications and have trouble gaining employment with a network television channel or radio station, try cable or public television, or work for the event planner who promotes the conferences for that television channel or radio station. Think of unexpected ways to solve the problem. Network, network, network!

Savings. Go to your credit union or bank and seek financial advice by calling the toll-free number for your 401(k) plan. You will be surprised by how much free information you receive. Try to develop a good relationship with your financial institution (which helps in emergencies). Your credit union or bank may provide seminars on how to purchase a home, save for retirement, and other financial planning topics for *free*. Take advantage of these classes; they are for you.

Taxes. Tax preparation can be costly. Go to www.irs.gov, https://locator.aarp.org/vmis/sites/tax_aide_locator.jsp, or your state or federal agency for free tax preparation. Call ahead to make sure you qualify for the free service and make an appointment. While you wait, write down all the questions you may have about increasing your tax deductions (e.g., homeownership or paying student loans). Please note that you are responsible for ensuring that you receive all your deductions.

Housing. Hardware and craft stores provide free classes on how to make minor home repairs (e.g., how to fix a running toilet). Take advantage of these classes; however, be cautious, as this is also a marketing strategy to persuade you to purchase tools. If you have a lot of home improvement needs, get on the store's mailing list for discounts or coupons. Decorating your home? Need home improvement, cannot afford retail prices, and do not mind used materials? To find a Habitat ReStores in your area visit www.habitat.org/env/restores.aspx).

Utilities and Cell Phone. Does your company affiliate with other companies such as club cards, utility or phone service? Find out by calling your human resources department. If not, call the utility or phone company for any specials.

Insurance (Health). When you go for your semiannual dental checkups, do you ask for sample toothpastes, toothbrushes, and dental floss? Contact lens solution samples are available at the optometrist. And pain relievers are available with your primary care physician. The samples are for you and may be used for travel.

Use this time to focus on the realities of your life and reevaluating your priorities. Thumb through everything you underlined or highlighted. Before you move to part 3, please take the time to make those changes now and look over appendixes 1 through 5. This is not a race; only you know your financial situation. You have already purchased this book, so get your money back by reducing your monthly bills.

Part III

The Results

Chapter 7

Be Creative

"Part I: The Beginning" described your current situation, and "Part II: The Breakthrough" helped you establish priorities and develop a budget, which allowed you to reduce some expenses. Hopefully you took the time to make those changes to reduce your monthly bills. If you did, by next month you will have saved the amount you paid for this book or more. You should feel better already. Now, "Part III: The Results" provides further options for long-lasting change (what to do, where to get information, and how to do it).

There is a learning curve in everything we do, but once you get into the swing of things, these changes will become second nature to you. And if you team up with someone, the changes will not seem so difficult. Please remember to consult with your financial advisor, especially if you make more than $600, which will require you to report your earnings to the IRS.

A variety of products are tested before they go on the market, such as coats, shoes, food, household products, and so on. When was the last time you bought some athletic shoes? Is your child outgrowing his or her shoes? Well, it does not take a rocket scientist to know that the cost of making an athletic shoe is a fraction of the actual market sales price. Professional basketball players provide affordable athletic gear. Please visit www.starbury.com.

If you are undecided about what clothing and shoes work best for your athletic activity and do not want to spend the money to find out, request to become a product tester for an athletic shoe company. Here are a few to get you started: become a product tester for Nike (https://producttesting.nike.com/producttest) or a wear tester for New Balance (http://weartest.newbalance.com). Or join Reebok's wear tester database—request a sports/fitness profile and mail your name, address, and phone number to Reebok International, Ltd., 1895 J W Foster Blvd., Canton, MA, 02021, Attn: Wear Test Department. Please note that testers are responsible for following the rules, filling out the survey, and returning the shoes after a period of time.

What if you could get an oil change and gas, go window shopping, eat out at a restaurant, and get reimbursed for the gas you used and the food you ate by receiving a check at the end of the month? Don't believe me? Try mystery shopping (free money). If you are receiving e-mails from a company regarding mystery shopping, it might be a scam; however, if you go to the actual Mystery Shopping Providers Association, www.mysteryshop.org/shoppers, this will help you start finding legitimate mystery shopping companies. Click on the companies provided and do your research. Some companies focus on certain regions of the country (e.g., North, South, East, West); some focus more on food than shopping; some require you to turn in your receipts, business cards, within twelve to twenty-four hours, and some do not. Whatever the requirements, pick a company that best fits your needs. Sign up for a username and password. Follow up if you do not receive any information on your username and password. Allow a month to receive your first paycheck. I recommend opening a new bank account for all mystery shopping pay. This can be your start for establishing an emergency fund.

Opening a new account? Do your research; some credit unions and banks offer up to $25 for opening a new account (free money). Sometimes you can receive a finder's fee for referring a friend. Just be careful to read the fine print.

Look around your home, room by room. Let's be honest: why are you holding on to the decorations you never used and shoes and clothes you never wore? Old silverware you never used? Old blinds you took down? What's in your attic? What is in your basement? What is in your jewelry box? The list can go on and on. Go room by room and clean house. Sell items on www.ebay.com, or have a yard sale (free money). As mentioned before, there is a learning curve. The first time you sell on eBay, do not be afraid to go through the tutorial or call the help line on setting up an account. Whatever you do not sell, donate to a local charity, and do not forget to get a receipt so you can claim the donation on your taxes.

A lot of college students give blood or plasma during the rough times, which can be a win-win situation. Not only are you helping to save a life, but you also get cash in your hand. But let's take this to another level. You know how you always hear about studies in the news? Well, where do the studies come from? Hospitals, universities, focus groups,. I would not recommend taking medications as part of a study, but the studies that want to monitor your eating habits or weight are easy. As a college student, I did a few studies that required me to be on a strict diet and measure my weight for a few weeks. Oh yeah, I forgot to tell you: the hospital provided the food and paid me $400 (free food and free money). Not bad, huh? Check with your hospital's research clinical trial department. Do not be discouraged if you get the runaround on the phone when you call the first time. Remember that the receptionist may be a temp who doesn't know where to direct the call. Just ask to speak with upper management in the research clinical trial department.

Do you have a lot to say? Want to voice your opinion? Well, you can get paid for that too. Pick up your local Sunday newspaper; don't just look at the coupons and advertisements, but read the newspaper in its entirety. People can get paid for writing about life moments or submitting pictures. For example, the *Washington Post* pays $100 to selected individuals who send a picture and less than one hundred words on life's pleasures in the Washington DC metropolitan area (free money).

Writing and taking pictures not your thing? What about your opinions? Sign up for a focus group. What is a focus group? A focus group is a marketing strategy for new products or services. The more education and/or experience you have, the better your chances to be selected for certain types of groups. Although participating in a focus group pays well, it often occurs during normal business hours (if you decide to take a day off, make sure the pay outweighs your regular rate of pay for that day). It is more difficult to find legitimate focus groups than to find studies. Look in the yellow pages, or surf the Internet for local focus groups in your area (free money). Do not expect to participate in a lot of focus groups (twice a year is great), because companies want to get a wide variety of opinions.

Did you get new contacts, buy new electronics, or buy certain foods with rebates? Well, did you turn in your rebates? Why not? Get into the habit of doing all your rebates the same day you purchase the product (free money). Although the rebate may take four to six weeks, that is money you did not have. This can be added to your emergency fund. Make copies for your records and mark your calendar; the money is coming.

Do you have an extra bedroom? Would it be too difficult to have a roommate for a few months (like an intern looking for a place to live) until you can get back on your feet? A deposit will prevent the roommate from skipping out on you. It's a sacrifice, but that sacrifice can help you get out of debt faster (free money).

We all have gifts. What is your gift? What service do you enjoy doing? Floral arranging, babysitting, and walking dogs are all self-satisfying activities that you can do to make a little extra money (free money).

Going green. Finally, it is cool to be environmentally conscious, so what are you doing to contribute to the planet's well-being? We waste too much material on a daily basis. Will it kill us to use a hand towel to wipe our hands in lieu of paper towels? Will it kill us to place a damp sponge in the microwave for a few seconds to kill the bacteria in order to reuse the sponge? Will it kill us to open the windows instead of running the air conditioner? Check out your local recycling centers for rebates. Place the money saved into a savings, CD, or money market account (free money).

These are just a few ways to make it happen. Metropolitan cities may have more focus groups, mystery shopping, or hospital opportunities. However, technology has made it easy for anyone—whether you are in a metropolitan area like Washington DC or a small town like Hopkinsville, Kentucky—to sell on eBay, receive rebates, or open a checking account online.

Refer to appendix 6 to help track your results.

Chapter 8

Make It Happen

Is your company doing well financially? Have you taken on more responsibility and been more productive by saving the company money? If you answered yes to those questions, know your worth (www.salary.com) and ask for a raise. If a raise is agreed upon, follow up in writing until you receive it. If a raise is not possible, negotiate for other perks like flex time, transportation tickets, or upgrades on your cell phone, computer, printer, Internet card, and so on.

By now, you have more than enough ways to reduce your expenses, create emergency options rather than using your credit card, and earn additional income without taxes being a huge burden. Now, what is your next step? Look for the unusual ideas; create more ways to save and make money and avoid falling back into bad habits. You cannot do it alone; bounce ideas off of family and friends. Get with one or two friends, and make it happen.

With all the money you are saving, use this season to explore creative ways to spend time with your loved ones. All too often we overlook so many opportunities that will make our life complete. Provided below are numerous free activities that are in front of our faces. Read the Bible, not because you are broke or bored, but to establish purpose in your life. I also recommend *The Purpose Driven Life* by Rick Warren. Participate in ministry with your church; this is a step to fulfill your purpose in life. Visit your local park, and observe the blessings of nature.

Want to go on vacation? Go on vacation in your city: visit the museums, go to the annual festivals, and enjoy the tourist attractions. Want to learn how to improve your home? Take a free hardware class. Want to enhance your knowledge of a variety of subjects? Take a free class online: visit www.ocw.mit.edu.

Open houses are ways to find new decorating ideas. Attend car, health, and technology conventions to get the latest information. For entertainment purposes only, attend a get-rich-scheme seminar. These can be very informative and sometimes provide a meal. Just be prepared to stay for a few hours and *just say no!* Attend art shows to enhance your knowledge of art. Volunteer for a worthy cause. Participate in your library activities. Do spring cleaning and cook a meal together as a family. With these ideas to keep you busy, it is your turn to be creative for more. This world is full of things to do, and the activities that do not cost anything are the most fulfilling.

With all the changes you have made in the last few months, it is important to turn these changes into a routine to sow good financial habits for your future. I believe in you!

Chapter 9

I Don't Pay My Bills;
I Have Others Pay My Bills

Congratulations! You have come a long way. If you followed the steps of living within your budget, reducing your expenses, and taking advantage of the many options available, then you are no longer paying on your bills, but you are having others pay your bills by being a mystery shopper, receiving free samples, or participating in a focus group.

As mentioned in "Chapter 1: The Real World," although we are loyal to our place of employment, corporate scandals and job security are issues everyone must take into consideration. *Never* depend on your job as your only source of income and savings for retirement. Think about it. Only the United States allows an average two-week vacation a year. People in other countries take multiple weeks or a few months off per year. With the work-related stress you go through year after year, not knowing whether your company will last until retirement is scary. I am not saying quit your job today; just open your mind to your dreams, your destiny, and your purpose. Create multiple sources of income.

You sat in the same classroom and learned the same subjects as everyone else who has a business. And let's be honest: you do all the work anyway. So why not start your own business? I know, you have to have money to start your own business. Well, that is where you do your research, get creative, and make it happen. Of course, I will not just give you all that information, because you may become my competition ☺; however, http://www.sbaonline.sba.gov/index.html or www.irs.gov will help you get started.

It is easy to say "Make It Happen," and believe me, in the past I never wanted my own business. It was only when I was at the company Christmas party and the company president mentioned all the countries he had visited that I realized I have never been outside of the country. Two weeks a year on my salary will not allow me to visit all these countries in my lifetime. I have been blessed in my life to be surrounded by family and friends who have their own businesses and encouraged me to do the same. But the light bulb just did not come on until that party. I kept my dream close to myself, told only a few, select, positive people, and started my research. Why can't you start your own business? When you open your own business, your life becomes so flexible, with more fulfilling life opportunities, not to mention the tax write-offs that help you succeed.

Conclusion

Other than how I manage my company, you have all the information I know. Now it is up to you how you use it. As mentioned before, this book is a source of general advice only. Please consult with your financial advisor before making any major financial decisions. Anchored 4 Generations, LLC, is not responsible for any losses, damages, or claims that may result from your financial decisions. If you are inspired to write a book, I recommend using iUniverse as your publisher. Please reference my book and name.

Appendixes

Appendix 1

Budget

In this example, the IRS Federal Tax Rate Schedule (refer to www.irs.gov for the most current information) places your annual income of $30,720 in a 28 percent tax bracket. Your gross pay is $2,560 per month, and your net (take-home) pay is $1,843.20 per month.

Monthly		Net	Actual
Tithes and Charity	10%	$184.32	$184.32
Savings	10%	$184.32	$5.00
Housing	30%	$552.96	$675.00
Utilities and Cell Phone	10%	$184.32	$92.79
Insurance (Car and Health)	5%	$92.16	$90.00
Transportation (Auto)	10%	$184.32	$350.00
Debt (e.g., Student Loans)	15%	$276.48	$125.00
Food	5%	$92.16	$250.00
Personal Care	2.5%	$46.08	$40.00

Monthly		Net	Actual
Recreation and Clothing	2.5%	$46.08	$129.00
Total	100%	$1,843.20	$1,941.11

The actual amount is unacceptable and will only take you deeper into debt.

Appendix 2

Sick and Tired

Gather all your bills and receipts. Write down all of your bills with their interest rates and monthly payments. Answer two questions: Is this bill in your budget? Can you pay it off this month?

Your net income: $ _____

Bill	Interest Rate	Monthly Payment	Remaining Balance	In Budget ?	Can this be paid off this month ?
Mortgage or Rent				Yes/No	Yes/No
Utilities				Yes/No	Yes/No
Home phone				Yes/No	Yes/No
Cell phone				Yes/No	Yes/No
Home Repair, Improvement				Yes/No	Yes/No

Bill	Interest Rate	Monthly Payment	Remaining Balance	In Budget ?	Can this be paid off this month ?
Insurances and Security				Yes/No	Yes/No
Tithes and Savings (401(k), Roth IRAs, CDs, etc.)				Yes/No	Yes/No
Medical Expenses				Yes/No	Yes/No
Credit Card #1				Yes/No	Yes/No
Credit Card #2				Yes/No	Yes/No
Credit Card #3				Yes/No	Yes/No
Loan #1				Yes/No	Yes/No
Loan #2				Yes/No	Yes/No
Food				Yes/No	Yes/No
Child Care				Yes/No	Yes/No
Child Expenses				Yes/No	Yes/No
Dry Cleaning				Yes/No	Yes/No
Gas				Yes/No	Yes/No

Bill	Interest Rate	Monthly Payment	Remaining Balance	In Budget?	Can this be paid off this month?
Car Insurance and Repair				Yes/No	Yes/No
Parking and Public Transportation				Yes/No	Yes/No
Entertainment				Yes/No	Yes/No
Personal (Salon, Barber, Clothing, Hygiene)				Yes/No	Yes/No
Other (e.g., Subscriptions)				Yes/No	Yes/No

Sick and Tired   Yes/No

Appendix 3

Negotiate Rent

Date

Via Facsimile and Certified Mail

Manager
Apartment Complex
Address
City, State, Zip

Manager's Name:

Subject: Your Address

It was a pleasure to meet with you yesterday. Per our conversation on day, date, please consider this letter as documentation to maintain the rent for (your address) in the amount of $XXX.XX. If possible, please provide confirmation this amount was agreed upon.

If you have any questions, please do not hesitate to contact me at
XXX-XXX-XXXX.

Thank you,

Name
E-mail
Phone

Appendix 4

Cancel PMI

Day, Date

Via Facsimile

Payment Processing
Your Mortgage Loan Company
Address
City, State Zip

ATTN: Payment Processing

To Whom It May Concern:

Subject: Private Mortgage Insurance (PMI) with Loan No. #

Please consider this letter a request to reanalyze my escrow account as well as my Private Mortgage Insurance (PMI) to estimate a lower mortgage monthly payment. As of day, date, my loan is at least two years old with the following: no payments of thirty days or more past due, no outstanding late charges, and no lender-paid mortgage insurance option.

The Homeowner's Protection Act (HPA), passed in 1999, mandates that lenders cancel mortgage insurance when the loan-to-value ratio reaches 22 percent.

Attached are estimates of the appreciated sold homes in my area, ranging from $XXX,XXX to $XXX,XXX. My current principal balance is approximately $XXX,XXX, which is approaching the loan-to-value ratio. Please advise my eligibility for my escrow account to be reanalyzed and my PMI to be canceled.

Thank you,

Name
E-mail
Phone

Appendix 5

Trim Those Expenses

Bill	Lowered interest rate	Reduced plan or option	Savings per month
Mortgage or Rent			
Utilities			
Home phone			
Cell phone			
Home Repair, Improvement			
Insurances and Security			
Tithes and Savings (401(k), Roth IRAs, CDs, etc.)			
Medical Expenses			
Credit Card #1			
Credit Card #2			
Credit Card #3			
Loan #1			
Loan #2			
Food			

Bill	Lowered interest rate	Reduced plan or option	Savings per month
Child Care			
Child Expenses			
Dry cleaning			
Gas			
Car Insurance and Repair			
Parking and Public Transportation			
Entertainment			
Personal (e.g., Salon, Barber, Clothing, Hygiene)			
Other (e.g., Subscriptions)			

Appendix 6

Be Creative

Options	Date Requested	Follow-Up	Results ($)
Employment (Asked for Raise)			
Product or Wear Tester			
Mystery Shopper #1			
Mystery Shopper #2			
Mystery Shopper #3			
Yard Sale			
eBay			
Research			
Newspaper or Magazines			
Focus Group			
Rebate #1			
Rebate #2			
Rebate #3			
Rent Out Room			
My Gift			
Recycling Center			

If you enjoyed this book, please recommend *Make It Happen in the Real World* for someone else.

Make It Happen in the Real World

A Practical Guide to Getting Your Finances in Order for Everyday People

By Tiffanie

To purchase additional books, please visit www.anchored4generations.com.

* Book ISBN 978-0-595-46416-4
* e-Book ISBN 978-0-595-90710-6

978-0-595-46416-6
0-595-46416-5